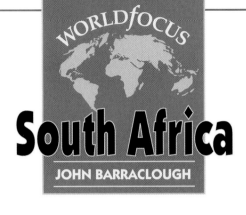

WORLDFOCUS

South Africa

JOHN BARRACLOUGH

Contents

Introduction

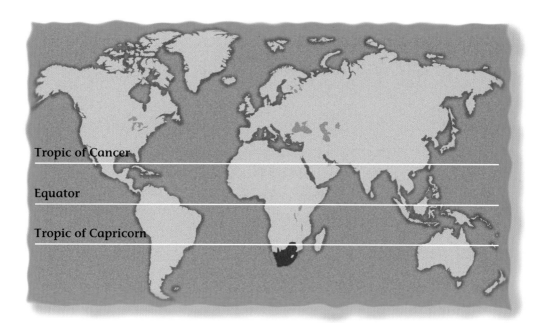

Tropic of Cancer

Equator

Tropic of Capricorn

When South Africa held elections in 1994 it was the first time that black South Africans had been able to vote. The African National Congress (ANC) won and Nelson Mandela was made president. His victory meant that **apartheid** was truly at an end.

△ **Where is South Africa?**

Apartheid

For nearly 300 years the white minority in South Africa had tried to rule the black majority using apartheid. The word 'apartheid' comes from the **Afrikaans** language and means 'separateness'. Apartheid laws declared that black people were not allowed to marry white people, nor were black and white people permitted to have children together. Blacks and whites had to go to different schools and only white people could vote.

Whites enjoyed good jobs and education, while most black people were made to live in '**homelands**' in the poorest parts of South Africa. In the homelands, black people lost all their legal rights under South African laws. They were paid low wages to work in white-owned mines, factories and farms. In the towns and cities blacks were forced by law to live in the worst areas.

▷ **There were huge celebrations when Nelson Mandela was made the first black president of South Africa.**

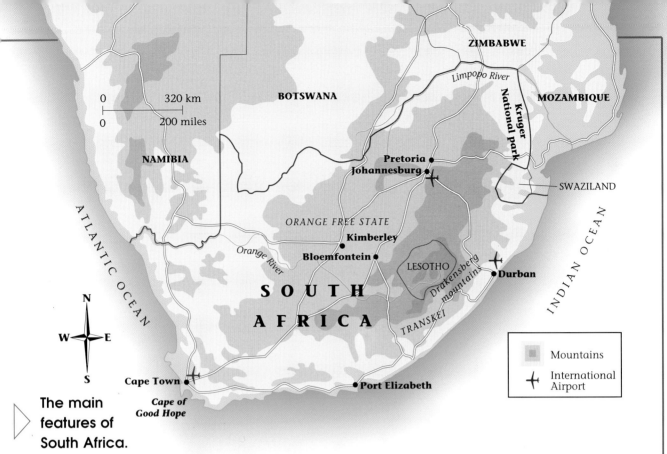

The main features of South Africa.

The end of apartheid

Most of the rest of the world thought apartheid was an evil system. Some countries put pressure on the South African government to stop it. They isolated South Africa through **sanctions** and stopped buying South African **exports** such as gold, diamonds and minerals, and food products. At the same time black organizations such as the ANC fought hard against apartheid. Many people involved in that fight, like Nelson Mandela, were put in prison. Faced with mounting international pressure and pressure from South Africans, President F W de Klerk realized that apartheid could not continue. Nelson Mandela had been in prison for 27 years before he was released in 1990, when F W de Klerk announced the end of apartheid and promised elections with 'one person, one vote'.

3

The people

The first people to live in the southern part of Africa were the San and the Koi-Koi. The San hunted animals and searched for plants to eat. The Koi-Koi kept animals and moved around the country, looking for the best grass for their herds of cattle, sheep and goats.

In the 17th century traders from Holland landed on the coast of southern Africa at a place they called the Cape of Good Hope. The settlement was a stop-off point for ships sailing from Europe to India and back. They called at the Cape for supplies and to pick up precious metals.

The British and Dutch

The **colonists** spread inland and in 1652 the first war broke out between the Dutch and the Koi-Koi. For the next 150 years there were many battles as local peoples fought first Dutch and then British settlers who wanted to take their land. By 1760 the Dutch colonists had crossed

There are 33 million blacks, Asians, and people of mixed race in South Africa and 5 million whites.

the Orange River. They were far from their home country and their language changed, influenced by Malay slaves, French and German settlers and San, Nguni and Koi-Koi peoples. A new language, **Afrikaans** came into being.

The British took control of the Cape in 1806. In 1834 some of the Dutch farmers (Boers) got into ox-carts and began the Great Trek north to find new land of their own. They travelled 1000 miles in two years and the Great Trek became an important part of Boer history.

The Boers and the British fought for control of the gold and diamond mining industries during the Boer War (1899–1902). Although the British won, they agreed to govern with the Dutch.

Gradually the white people took away black people's rights and forced them to leave their families' land and live in the poorest parts of the country. At the same time the white people needed workers. Black men were sent to work in the white mines and factories, and Indian workers and merchants were brought to the country.

Black people, including Indians, were treated unfairly and often cruelly, but, without the right to vote, they couldn't change things through the political system. Instead they campaigned and struggled, often secretly. Many people risked their lives fighting **apartheid**.

▽ Many black townspeople live without piped water or electricity.

Apartheid is over in South Africa. Now the descendants of the British and Dutch, the black Africans and the Asians are living with the problems it left behind.

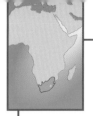

Where do people live?

South Africa is five times the size of the UK and has about two-thirds the population. Most of the centre of the country is a high, dry plateau.

Because South Africa is very big it has different climates in different parts of the country. The west is almost desert. In the east are the Drakensberg mountains (see map page 3) that drop down to the coastal plain. Here sugar, tea and wood for timber grow well. The south, around Cape Town, is like the Mediterranean. Winters are mild and the summers are hot. It is perfect for growing grapes, and wine is a major export.

More than half of South Africa's 38 million people live in the towns and cities such as Cape Town, Durban and Johannesburg.

▽ **Cape Town. South Africa has big, sophisticated cities.**

▽ Black people's housing was deliberately neglected under apartheid.

Apartheid shaped where people live in South Africa more than anything else. Under the Group Areas Act of 1950 towns were divided into 'low-income' zones for blacks, and 'high-income' areas with better houses for whites. Under **pass laws** black people could only go into white areas if they carried a pass.

Homelands

Apartheid also gave the police powers to move black people by force onto South Africa's worst land. These places were called **homelands**. All blacks – 80 per cent of the population – were expected to live in the homelands, unless they had permission to live in the **townships**. The homelands made up only one-tenth of the country's area.

More than three million black people were moved by force to the homelands before apartheid ended. They were overcrowded, too many trees were cut down, and the soil became useless for farming.

Now that apartheid has ended, people are leaving these areas. Some are trying to go back to their old land, and many young people are moving to the townships, such as Soweto, to look for work. But jobs and housing are in very short supply in South Africa and new arrivals often end up as **squatters**, living on the edge of the city in self-made shacks. Three-quarters of black townspeople live without running water, proper **sanitation** or electricity.

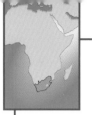

Agriculture

South African fruit, vegetables and wines are **exported** all over the world. Apples, oranges, pineapples and almost any other crops grow well because the soil is mostly fertile and there is a good mix of rain and sunshine all year round.

△ In some country areas the soil is poor and farming is difficult.

Wheat is grown in the centre and south west, and the big areas of grassland are good for raising cattle and sheep. In most years South Africa exports more food than it **imports**. But in 1991 one of the worst droughts of the century hit the whole of southern Africa. Harvests were poor and that year South Africa had to buy more food from other countries than it sold abroad.

Farm workers

Under **apartheid** more than three-quarters of the land was reserved for whites, including the best farmland. Black farm workers were paid very low wages and had no right to join a union to fight for better working conditions. Often their houses belonged to the farm owners and they could be thrown out at any time.

▷ Farm workers carrying grapes to make wine.

Even though apartheid is over, not much has changed yet on South Africa's farms and vineyards. Most are still owned by white people, with black people doing most of the work. But black people are now free to travel and many are leaving the white farms to go to the **townships** to look for work. Others are losing their jobs because farming machines are replacing the people who used to cut the crops.

In the 1960s and 1970s three million blacks were forced to resettle in the **homelands**, some of the worst agricultural land in the country. The hills soon became bare. Now the rain washes away the fertile topsoil and cuts deep channels called **dongas** which make ploughing very difficult.

Most of the farms in the old homelands are smallholdings. A family might keep a few chickens or a cow, and grow maize which is called **mealies** in South Africa.

▽ Pineapples are just one of the many types of fruit exported by South Africa.

Industry

South Africa's biggest industry is mining. It produces more gold and diamonds than any other country and gold is the most important **export**. Some of the gold mines have shafts over 3 km (2 miles) deep. As you go down a mine the temperature rises because you get nearer to the hot centre of the Earth. It is very hot and dangerous working deep in the gold mines. Safety standards are poor and accidents are common.

Most miners are black and live in hostels near the mines. Women and children were not allowed at the hostels and men could be away from their families for years. The black **townships** which have grown up around the mines and factories are badly affected by pollution of the air and water.

Diamonds

Diamonds were discovered at a place called Kimberley (see map page 3) in the Orange Free State in 1867. They were important in South Africa's early development. The money from selling diamonds paid for roads and

△ **Most of the underground work in South Africa's mines is done by black mineworkers.**

new buildings. Today the Kimberley mine is the biggest artificial hole in the world. Thirty million tonnes of earth were dug out to find just three tonnes of diamonds. South Africa also produces and exports coal, iron, platinum, manganese and asbestos.

SAFETY HAT AREA
VEILIGHEIDSHELM
GEBIED

Tourism

Now that **apartheid** is over, more tourists are visiting the country and tourism is being encouraged by the government. It is becoming a very important source of income. Most visitors go to enjoy the beautiful scenery, sandy beaches and wildlife parks. Kruger National Park has lions, elephants, zebras, and lots of other animals including an antelope only found wild in South Africa: the springbok.

When South Africa was isolated by many other countries of the world because of apartheid, it had to develop its own industries. The arms (weapons) industry grew to be one of its strongest. South Africa used its military strength to occupy nearby Namibia and was involved in wars with some of its neighbours, including Mozambique and Angola. South Africa is now a major exporter of weapons to other countries.

▽ Tourism is important for South Africa's economy. The country's excellent beaches are one reason holiday-makers go there.

Challenges

△ **In the townships people often have to collect water from taps in the street.**

For more than 300 years a small number of white people, the minority, **discriminated** against black people, the majority, in South Africa. The black population was deliberately kept poor and under-educated. The white government and employers saw them as a big, cheap workforce that could be controlled. It was a very unfair society and **apartheid** made things worse by making the discrimination legal.

Black people were forced by law to live in the poorest parts of the country and to go to the worst schools, and they couldn't get good jobs. The system made South Africa one of the most divided countries in the world.

Cities

There are huge differences between the lives of rich and poor people, and white and black people, in South Africa. Most white people live in cities such as Johannesburg, Cape Town and Durban. They are usually richer than black people. Almost all whites have taps and toilets in their houses. But more than half of the black population don't have decent **sanitation**.

Apartheid also made a big difference to how long people live. White people have a **life expectancy** of 73 years. Black people can expect to live to 63. In the UK the life expectancy is 76.

More and more schools have mixed (black and white) classes. This was illegal under apartheid.

Since the election of a **democratic** government in 1994, South Africa has changed. Apartheid has ended, and people are hoping for a more peaceful and prosperous future.

Housing and education

More than three million black people were thrown off their land under apartheid. Now they want it back, but can't afford to buy it from the new owners. There is also a big shortage of houses. One black person in six lives in a self-made shack without running water.

There is a lot of pressure on the new government to solve these problems and provide people with better education and jobs. But the biggest challenge facing all South Africans is how to make sure people of all races respect each other after so many years of mistrust. Everyone will have to work together to create a society in which everyone has the same opportunities in life.

Marconi Beam

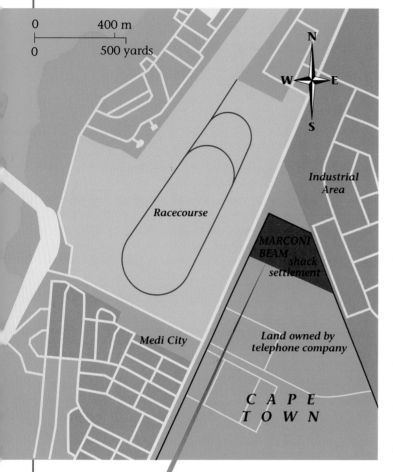

Marconi Beam is a small shack settlement in the north of Cape Town, near the coast. Cape Town is the second biggest city in South Africa. Nearly two million people live in the city and its suburbs.

The land on which Marconi Beam is built is owned by a telephone company. People have been living on this land illegally, as squatters, since the 1960s. Then, many of the men worked at nearby stables. The men could have lived at the stables but because of the **pass laws** of **apartheid** their wives and children would not have been allowed to join them. So the men chose to live with their families in self-made shacks at Marconi Beam.

Shacks

The shacks were made from waste wood, plastic and corrugated iron. Houses often burned down because there was no electricity and people cooked on open fires or paraffin stoves.

From time to time the police tried to move the families off the land. The shacks were destroyed and people lost all their possessions, but each time they came back.

In 1986 the pass laws were stopped and lots of people moved to the cities to look for work. Marconi Beam grew because it was near a main road and the city centre. By 1990 it was home to 250 families.

△ Marconi Beam grew on unused land near the city centre. From here it was easy for people to walk to work in the city.

At the same time, apartheid was ending and black people were able to plan more for their futures. The Marconi Beam residents set up a civic association. They wanted decent living conditions, **sanitation** and electricity, and the legal right to live on the land and to build brick houses. The community bargained with the telephone company and the council for three years until they got most of what they asked for, including ownership of the land.

▽ Waiting for school to open in the morning.

Now there are more than a thousand homes at Marconi Beam and living conditions have improved. Some families have built new houses and the council have put taps in most streets to provide water. But it is still an unhealthy and difficult place to live. The shacks are too hot in summer and cold and wet in winter. Most people still do not have brick houses, running water or electricity.

▷ Shacks in Marconi Beam are made from whatever people can find – wooden crates, plastic sheeting, corrugated iron.

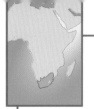

Life in Marconi Beam

Marconi Beam is close to a fast growing industrial part of Cape Town. This is why a lot of people came to live in the area. Some people from the community work in the nearby factories but there is still a lot of unemployment. Half the residents do not have a full-time job.

A yellow blanket of smoke covers the houses on days when there is no wind. It is pollution from an oil refinery and a fertilizer factory in the industrial area. Chest illnesses are common in Marconi Beam and the pollution can make people feel worse.

Health

Once a week a mobile clinic from a neighbouring suburb visits the community to treat women and children. All the treatment and all of the medicines are free. The nurses treat a lot of children with diarrhoea and people with the chest disease **tuberculosis**. Diarrhoea can be very dangerous for small children because they can die from losing lots of water from their bodies.

In South Africa people often go to a traditional healer, or **gqirha**, when they are ill. Every healer has a special name. They are respected and even small children always call them by their healer name.

Wadlagaza is a healer in Marconi Beam, though she grew up in the Transkei in the east. It takes a long time to qualify as a gqirha. Wadlagaza began her training when she was 18 but she did not qualify until she was 33 years old.

▽ Small, local shops are called spazas.

She had to learn the names and uses of 5000 medicinal plants. Sometimes she goes back to the Transkei to collect plants that do not grow in the area around Cape Town.

As well as curing illnesses, healers also help to keep people healthy by suggesting nutritious food to eat, for example. The government has registered all healers as **primary health workers**. When the Marconi Beam community hall opened, healers led the celebrations by performing traditional dances.

△ Wadlagaza, a traditional healer, mixing herbs to make medicine.

School

Schools were **segregated** during the **apartheid** years, so that black and white pupils did not mix. Nearly 20 times more money was spent on white children than on black children. There were shortages of classrooms, teachers and books for black children and many of their schools were left in a poor state of repair. It left a quarter of the population **illiterate**, unable to read or write. Now the new, **democratic**, government is trying to make education fairer. They want everyone to go to school for at least ten years.

The Elda Mahlentle School

The school at Marconi Beam is named after the headmistress and person who started it, Ms Elda Mahlentle. She saw that many children were not going to school because their families were too poor to afford the travelling costs to other parts of Cape Town. So she raised money in the community and also asked people to give books and equipment. After two years the school was ready. Now the government pays the teachers and provides textbooks.

▽ The people of Marconi Beam raised money to build their own school.

△ Children have to pass exams at the end of each year, before they can go up to the next year.

There are 400 pupils and 12 teachers at the Elda Mahlentle school. Most children walk to school and some are collected by a local businessman and taxi owner, Mr Ncalo. The main school building is made from eight truck containers.

Lessons

Pupils learn to read and write in Xhosa, an African language, and in English in their first two years. Each year after that is called a **standard**. Children study ten standards in all. The Elda Mahlentle school teaches up to standard six. The pupils study Xhosa, English, **Afrikaans**, maths, geography, science, history and agriculture.

In the Elda Mahlentle school the day starts at 8 a.m. when everybody lines up outside. Before classes start they sing a hymn and teachers read from the Bible. There are 15-minute breaks at 10 a.m. and 12.30 a.m. School finishes at 2 p.m. On Fridays the pupils spend the last two lessons tidying their classrooms. Most children wear a uniform but some families cannot afford them. Once a week the whole school walks one and a half kilometres to a field to play netball and football.

Spare time

Going to church is a very important part of life in Marconi Beam. There are lots of different churches and they hold meetings most evenings. People go to church to meet each other and to chat, as well as to worship. Each church has its own choir and the services involve lots of singing and some dancing.

There is also a youth choir. The members are either high school students or they have left school and are looking for jobs. The choir practises every night and enters talent competitions.

Sport

Sport is taken very seriously in South Africa. The national rugby and cricket teams are world class and football is very popular. When the rest of the world cut links with South Africa because of **apartheid**, their teams could not compete with other countries. South Africa was banned from the Olympics and the Commonwealth Games until **sanctions** were lifted.

▽ Mrs Madolo goes to community meetings to discuss how to get better facilities in Marconi Beam.

Now the country's sports teams are taking part in competitions around the world again.

In Marconi Beam people play football and netball where they can, on spare ground. There are no proper sports pitches in the neighbourhood. The football teams play and train on the beach. The boxing club trains at the community hall in the evenings.

The hall is also used for political and community meetings.

All kinds of issues are discussed, such as the new brick houses or how to get more books for the school. There are no meetings at the weekend because this is when the shopping and household chores are done.

△ Boxing is popular in Marconi Beam. Asanda and Vuziyalo go to the local club to train in the evenings or to the beach in the daytime.

Shebeens and shops

When the meetings are over, people might go to a **shebeen** to carry on talking and to have a drink. A shebeen is like a pub. It sells beer and stronger drinks but does not have a licence. Shebeens are found all over South Africa and during the day most shebeens are **spaza** shops. These are shops that a family runs from home. Some only sell a few things, like candles, salt, cool drinks and flour. Others are like small supermarkets.

A day with the Madolo family

△ Vuziyalo leaves the house at seven to go to school.

The Madolo family is like many others living in South Africa's towns and cities. It is a single parent family, with Mrs Siniwe Madolo looking after three children and two grandchildren in the same shack. Women on their own look after nearly a quarter of the homes in Marconi Beam. This is usually because the men are away working, or have abandoned their families.

Mrs Madolo's husband, Macebo, spent two years in prison in the 1960s for being a member of a political party that was banned at the time. In prison he was hit on the head and never fully recovered. He died in 1981.

Mrs Madolo has had a difficult life. Her eldest son Peter also died in 1981 in a car crash. Then a big fire in 1994 destroyed several shacks in Marconi Beam. The Madolo house burned to the ground and the family lost everything, including all the photographs of their father. Mrs Madolo's sewing machine was saved though, and she can still earn a little money by sewing.

The day

Vuziyalo, Mrs Madolo's youngest son, is the first person up in the morning. He is in **standard** seven and goes to school outside Marconi Beam. Most days he catches a minibus taxi and has left the house by 7 a.m. As he is leaving, Patricia, Mrs Madolo's daughter, gets up with her niece Bulelwa and nephew Asanda. They all share a room with Mrs Madolo. They have **mealie** porridge for breakfast and the four of them leave home by 7.45 a.m. The children go to school and Mrs Madolo goes to the community hall to look after nursery children.

The only person left in the house is Thombizodwa, Mrs Madolo's second daughter. She shares a room with Vuziyalo. She does not have a paid job at the moment and so she does most of the housework, shopping and cooking. Bulelwa and Patricia come home from school at 2 p.m. They wash their school shirts for the next day, have lunch and then play outside or do homework.

Evening

In the evenings Asanda and Vuziyalo go to the boxing club after they have swept the yard. Before supper, around 7 p.m., someone has to fetch water from the nearest tap. The children take turns to do this. After supper the family sits and talks while Mrs Madolo does her sewing. Once a week she goes to a community development meeting. By 10 p.m. everybody is in bed.

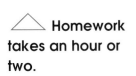 Homework takes an hour or two.

▷ Mrs Madolo at the nursery, where she works in the daytime.

Travel around Marconi Beam

There are a few cars in Marconi Beam and some bicycles, but most people walk to get to where they want to go. Most things people need are within walking distance. Every morning the place is busy with lots of people walking. They walk to school, to work, to get water from a tapstand, to the community hall and to the beach a few kilometres away. One reason Marconi Beam grew is because it is near a main road and close to the centre of Cape Town.

Minibuses

For longer distances people use minibus taxis. Mr Zwelethu Ncalo owns three minibuses. He came to Cape Town in 1971 from the Transkei. For years he worked as a petrol pump attendant and as a driver. Eventually he saved enough money to start his own business, a **spaza** shop, selling paraffin, sugar, sweets, bread and salt.

▽ Mr Ncalo hopes to open a supermarket in Marconi Beam.

 Minibus taxis are popular all over South Africa. They are cheap and fast.

The shop is named after his wife, Nobantu, and is also the Marconi Beam post office.

Mr Ncalo also owns a **shebeen** and has become a big businessman in the community. Early every morning he drives one of his minibuses to neighbouring settlements to pick up children who go to school in Marconi Beam.

Minibuses are used all over South Africa and most black people depend on them for getting around. They are cheap but they have a reputation for being dangerous. Many are not run legally and to make more money their drivers cram in as many passengers as they can. Often a minibus taxi will not leave a place until it is completely full. Then they drive very fast to beat other taxis to where they are going. There is fierce competition between rival taxi companies and sometimes this can become violent and turn into a 'taxi war'.

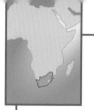

Travel around South Africa

South Africa has a very good main road system that criss-crosses the country, linking towns and cities and connecting South Africa to neighbouring countries. Long-distance buses travel along these routes between cities like Cape Town and Johannesburg, a distance of 1500 km. The buses are even quicker than the trains.

Trains

Like most other things under **apartheid**, trains were also **segregated** into whites-only and blacks-only carriages. A black person could not sit next to a white person. There were first, second, and third class carriages and white people were not allowed to travel in third class. This was the cheapest and reserved for black people only. Today, all South Africans can sit where they want on trains.

Some of the railways run through beautiful scenery. Tourists come from all over the world to travel on the famous Blue Train which runs between Cape Town and Johannesburg.

▽ Most towns have a busy taxi station and the minibuses race each other to get most passengers.

△ South Africa's famous Blue Train. South Africa's railway system was built by the British.

People on the move

A lot of people have moved around South Africa in the last few years. Often men left the rural areas to work in mines and factories at the other side of the country. Some would only be able to return home once a year. People are still moving to the towns to look for work.

At weekends there is a lot of travelling as people go home to visit their families and then return to the cities to work on Monday. Most people going home for the weekend travel by minibus or long distance bus. Travellers also get around by hitch-hiking.

Now that other countries are doing business with South Africa again because apartheid has ended, the national airline is flying to other African countries. *South African Airlines* fly regularly to and from Europe and the USA.

Looking at South Africa

South Africa

A dramatic mountain range in the east of the country.

Traditional clothing is often worn on special occasions and for ceremonies.

South Africa has changed greatly in the last few years. Before 1990, 5 million white people had tried to rule more than 30 million black people through the **apartheid** system.

Apartheid was a **racist** system because it deliberately tried to stop black people's development. Apartheid shaped South Africa from top to bottom. It touched everybody's lives and made black and white people think and behave badly towards each other.

Now apartheid is over and there is a freely elected black majority government. People all over the world celebrated when Nelson Mandela was made president of the 'new' South Africa. They were full of hope and optimism for a better future for all South Africans.

In some ways South Africa is a completely different country and a changed society. Black people have the same rights as white people for the first time in more than 300 years.

▷ Young people expect a better future in the 'new' South Africa, now that apartheid has ended.

But in other ways things have not changed at all. South Africa is still a divided country. The people of Marconi Beam still live in shacks and there is still a huge difference between the lives of the people in the **squatter** camps and the smart houses of Cape Town. The lives and opportunities of the poor are still greatly limited.

▽ Semi-desert on the border with Namibia.

The legacy of apartheid is the major challenge facing all South Africans today. To give all its people an equal chance of decent lives, South Africa needs to change even more than it has done already.

South Africa

Glossary

Afrikaans The language spoken by **Afrikaners**, and by other groups mainly around Cape Town.

Afrikaner A white South African, descended from the original Dutch settlers.

Apartheid The system of 'separate development' used by the white government to try to make black people's lives inferior to whites.

Colonists Groups of settlers who left their own homes to live in new lands under the rule of their old countries.

Commute To travel to work.

Democratic A democratic country has a government which has been freely elected by the people. Adults vote at an election for the government of their choice.

Discriminate To treat a person unfairly because they are different in some way, such as in their choice of religion or their skin colour.

Donga A gully in the earth caused by rain cutting into bare soil.

Exports Goods which are sold to other countries.

Gqirha A traditional healer in South Africa.

Homelands Under apartheid 13 per cent of South Africa was set aside for all black people (80 per cent of the population). These areas were called 'homelands' by the government.

Imports Goods bought in from other countries.

Illiterate To be unable to read and write.

Life expectancy The age someone can expect to live to.

Mealie Maize (corn on the cob).

Pass laws The apartheid laws that controlled where black people lived and how they moved around were called pass laws. Under these laws all blacks had to carry a pass book at all times.

Primary health worker Trained person who encourages basic health awareness and education that aims to keep people healthy.

Racist Someone who believes they are superior to other people because of the colour of their skin.

Sanctions When a country or countries deliberately stop trading with another country to force it to change.

Sanitation The disposal of refuse and sewage in drains and sewers.

Segregation To divide people into groups based on their religion, or colour, or beliefs.

Shebeen A bar selling alcohol without permission.

Spaza A shop run from someone's home.

Squatters People who live on someone else's property, usually because they have nowhere else to live.

Standard A school year in South Africa.

Townships Separate areas for black people on the edge of white towns. Soweto is a township on the edge of Johannesburg.

Tuberculosis A disease of the lungs, often caught in poor, overcrowded places.

Index

About Oxfam in South Africa

The international family of Oxfam organizations works with poor people and their organizations in over 70 countries. Oxfam believes that all people have basic rights: to earn a living, and to have food, shelter, health care, and education. Oxfam provides relief in emergencies, and gives long-term support to people struggling to build a better life for themselves and their families.

Oxfam UK and Ireland's programme in South Africa aims particularly to support the forces for social change in South Africa, and to bear witness to the poverty and oppression left by apartheid. Oxfam works with the most marginalized sections of society, helping them to take control of the processes that affect their lives: rural communities driven from their land and those struggling in the impoverished homelands, farm workers and their families, squatter communities, and women. In the country's current fluid political situation, Oxfam also supports initiatives to influence debate and policy on land reform, sustainable land use, workers' rights, and urban renewal.

The publishers would like to thank the following for their help in preparing this book: the staff of the Southern Africa desk; Stephen Morrow and the staff of the Oxfam office in Johannesburg; the Development Action Group in Cape Town who gathered the information on Marconi Beam, the Madolo family and the people of Marconi Beam; Mary Patience of Oxfam's Education Staff in Scotland who commented on early drafts.

The Oxfam Education Catalogue lists a range of other resources on economically developing countries, including South Africa, and issues of development. These materials are produced by Oxfam, by other agencies, and by Development Education Centres. For a copy of the catalogue contact Oxfam, 274 Banbury Road, Oxford OX2 7DZ, phone (01865) 311311, or your national Oxfam office.

Photographic acknowledgements

The author and publishers wish to acknowledge, with thanks, the following photographic sources:

Ruth Versfeld pp11, 28; Eye Ubiquitous p3; John Baguley p6; Matthew Sherrington pp7, 8, 9, 15, 29; Hutchison Library p9b; SouthLight pp10, 13, 26; Nancy Durrell-McKenna pp12, 29r; Robert Harding p27; Gill de Vlieg p4; all other photos are by Paul Grendon

The publishers have made every effort to trace the copyright holders, but if they have inadvertently overlooked any, they will be pleased to make the necessary arrangement at the first opportunity.

Cover photograph: SouthLight Photo Agency and Library, South Africa

Note to the reader - In this book there are some words in the text which are printed in **bold** type. This shows that the word is listed in the glossary on page 30. The glossary gives a brief explanation of words which may be new to you.

First published in Great Britain by Heinemann Library an imprint of Heinemann Publishers (Oxford) Ltd Halley Court, Jordan Hill, Oxford OX2 8EJ

OXFORD LONDON EDINBURGH MADRID ATHENS BOLOGNA PARIS MELBOURNE SYDNEY AUCKLAND SINGAPORE TOKYO IBADAN NAIROBI HARARE GABORONE PORTSMOUTH NH (USA)

© 1995 Heinemann Publishers (Oxford)

00 99 98 97 96 95
10 9 8 7 6 5 4 3 2 1

British Library Cataloguing in Publication Data
Barraclough, John
    South Africa – (Worldfocus Series)
    I. Title II. Series
    968

ISBN 0 431 07269 8 (Hardback)

ISBN 0 431 07268 X (Paperback)

Designed and produced by Visual Image
Cover design by Threefold Design

Printed in Hong Kong

A 5% royalty on all copies of this book sold by Heinemann Publishers (Oxford) Ltd will be donated to Oxfam (United Kingdom and Ireland), a registered charity number 202918.